ANIMALS of Long Ago

by Susan Ring / illustrated by Will Nelson

Chapters

SCHOLASTIC INC.
New York   Toronto   London   Auckland   Sydney
Mexico City   New Delhi   Hong Kong   Buenos Aires

Developed by Kirchoff/Wohlberg, Inc., in cooperation with Scholastic Inc.

Age of Fishes

Our world has been around for many, many, MANY years. Have you ever wondered what the world was like long ago? What animals were around?

Let's go way back in time. Put on your diving suit. You are going under water!

It is the Age of Fishes, about 370 million years ago. Down on the ocean floor, you see something that looks like a yellow flower. It is an animal called a *crinoid*. It is related to starfish we see in the ocean today.

You see something else that looks like a plant. But it's not. It's coral. Coral is made of tiny animal skeletons.

You finally see an animal that looks like an animal. It looks like a bug. It has a hard shell and two antennae. It is a *trilobite*. Its name does not mean it will bite you. It means that its body is divided into three parts. Most trilobites were about an inch long. Some grew as long as two feet.

3

Something big swims past, so big you feel the water push against you. It has big jaws too, but no teeth. This fish is covered with bony plates. It looks like it is wearing armor. It also looks a little like a shark. Then you see another fish. This one looks exactly like a shark. It IS a shark! Let's get out of the water and look for animals on land. Notice that the land is mostly bare. There are a few plants and short trees, but no animals. Wait! Something on the ground just moved.

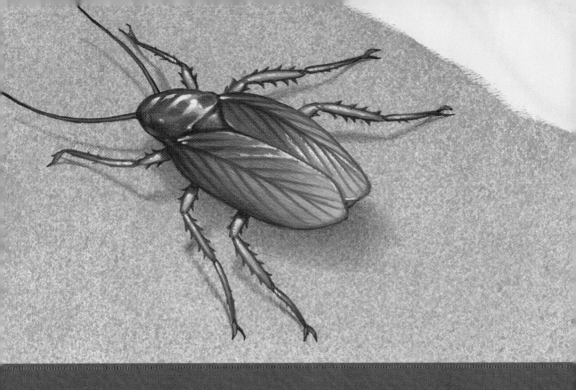

You bend down for a look. It is an insect. It has a flat body and a hard shell. It has spiny legs and two antennae. You look closer and see two wings. The wings are as long as the body. It's a cockroach! You are looking at one of Earth's very first insects!

You look for more animals, but there aren't any—yet. As we continue on our time trip, trilobites and armored fish will become extinct. They will die out. Sharks and cockroaches are still with us, though. They have changed very little since those times.

Age of Insects

To find more land animals, you jump ahead 70 million years. It is now the Age of Insects. There are other animals here, too.

You are in a forest with very tall trees. They look different than the trees of your time. There are also many plants. A lot of them look different, too. You recognize a few plants as giant ferns. The air is warm. You feel sticky.

You look down at your shoe. A brown insect runs across your foot. It hides under a fern. What was that?

You look closely at the fern and spot the insect. It has a hard body and a flat shell. It looks just like—well, a cockroach! They are still around, somehow. They didn't become extinct when many of the fishes did. While you are looking at the cockroach you hear a sound above you. You look up.

Whew! Something big flies by. You follow it to see what it is.

It is a giant dragonfly. Its wings are three feet across! It's the biggest insect on Earth.

The dragonfly has led
you to a small pool of water.
There are more animals here.
One is a snake. Another looks like a
lizard. You are seeing one of Earth's
first reptiles!

A giant millipede crawls up to the
pond. It has legs up and down both
sides. It must be three feet long! There's
no way you could step on this insect!

Most of the animals you see here will be
gone at your next stop. In time, all of these
trees and lush plants will turn into coal.

Age of Dinosaurs

Would you like to see a dinosaur? Some were as small as chickens, while others were giants. Some of them walked on land. Some swam. Others flew. Dinosaurs lived from 200 to 65 million years ago.

You decide to go to 85 million years ago. You are standing near a pond. There is no sign of a dinosaur or any animals, except . . . that cockroach over there. It hears a sound and runs under a rock. You look up. A whole herd of dinosaurs—big ones—is coming.

You run behind some big rocks. From there, you watch a herd of triceratopses come to the water. They have three sharp horns on their heads. You are not worried. They eat plants, not meat.

Then, out comes the biggest beast you have ever seen. It has a huge mouth full of big teeth. The ground shakes with its every step.

This is a tyrannosaurus rex. It circles the triceratopses, watching their horns. You don't have horns. Get out of there!

Age of Mammals

You jump ahead. The dinosaurs are gone. You land now in the Age of Mammals. This age lasted from about 2 million to 10 thousand years ago. Huge areas of ice came and went during a number of ice ages.

First you visit land that is not under the ice. You see huge animals that look like beavers. Did you shrink? No, these truly are giant beavers. They weigh about 400 pounds. That's as much as a gorilla! Here come two more big, furry animals. They walk on their knuckles. They are 20 feet long!

These are ground sloths. They can easily reach into the treetops for food. Their long tails help them stand up. One carries a baby on her back. These are not like the sloths of today that hang upside down from trees. These sloths would break a tree branch if they did that!

You jump to a different place. The first animal you see is sitting on your jacket. You know this one. It's another cockroach! Brush it off. Look for something else.

There's something big and hairy over there by that tree. You move forward and stop behind a skinny tree. The shaggy monster has four thick legs. It has a trunk like an elephant. It's a mastodon. Then you notice something sneaking up on it. This is a big cat with two huge teeth. It is a saber-toothed cat.

Saber-toothed cats could bring down a mastodon. The cat stops creeping. Now it looks at your tree. Mastodons and saber-toothed cats will become extinct. You decide not to wait for that to happen. You move on.

Ice covers much of the land where you are now. There are not many trees here. The cold has killed a lot of them.

You see a woolly rhino. Then you hear a loud sound, like the trumpet of an elephant.

Instead, it is a woolly mammoth. It is even taller than an elephant. Its shaggy fur keeps it warm. It uses its long tusks to look under the snow for small plants to eat.

Many animals could not bear the cold, though. Some moved to warmer places. Many died out completely. It's time for you to come back to today. We live in the Age of Man. It started out about ten thousand years ago.

Almost all the animals you saw on your trip back through time are gone now. How do we know they ever really lived?

Many people like to dig into the past. They REALLY dig! They dig to find fossils. A fossil can be a bone, an animal track, or a leaf print in stone. It can be part of an animal that turned to stone. It can be an insect in amber. Some insects got stuck in tree sap. Over time, the sap got hard. This became amber.

Fossils are proof that these animals once lived. Animal bones can be put together. They can show how the animal looked and moved.

Some people think archaeologists hunt fossils. They do not. They learn how people lived long ago. The archaeologists look through ruins for pottery and cloth. Scientists who study fossils are called paleontologists.

Some of the animals you saw are still alive. Sharks still swim in the oceans. And that thing crawling across this page? Yes, cockroaches are still with us! They seem to share a secret to survival. You might say cockroaches really know how to live. We don't know exactly why some animals died and some lived.

Paleontologists look for more fossils every day. They are looking for new information to teach us more secrets of the past.